BIRD VIEWING AREAS

Forests
Crops
Livestock
Other

Often underrated for its wildlife, Sweden's vast forests, thousands of pristine lakes and remote Lapland are the permanent or temporary home of 534 species of birds including 25 that are globally threatened. The world famous birding hotspot at Falsterbo is a must to see in the fall when an estimated 500 million birds pass through on migration.

Most illustrations show the adult male in breeding coloration. Colors and markings may be duller or absent during different seasons. The measurements denote the length of species from bill to tail tip. Illustrations are not to scale.

978-1-62005-350-8 $7.95 U.S.
ISBN
UPC
8 84682 01332 6
10 9 8 7 6 5 4 3 2 1
Made in the USA

SWEDEN BIRDS

A Folding Pocket Guide to Familiar Species

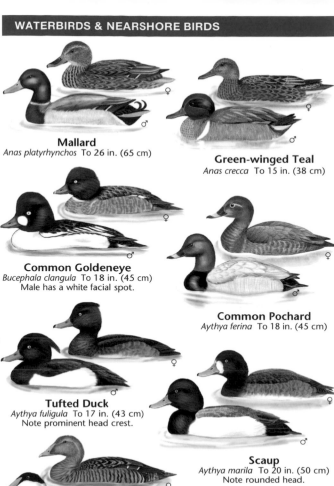

SWEDEN BIRDS – A Folding Pocket Guide to Familiar Species   Kavanagh/Leung

T0123975

Red-throated Loon
Gavia stellata
To 25 in. (63 cm)
Winter / Summer

Arctic Loon
Gavia arctica To 27 in. (68 cm)
Note white flank patch.
Winter / Summer

Little Grebe
Tachybaptus ruficollis
To 12 in. (30 cm)
Winter / Summer

Great Crested Grebe
Podiceps cristatus To 20 in. (50 cm)
Winter / Summer

Whooper Swan
Cygnus cygnus
To 5 ft. (1.5 m)
Yellow bill is black tipped.
Has a whooping call.

Mute Swan
Cygnus olor
To 5 ft. (1.5 m)
Has a pronounced knob on its orange beak.

Graylag Goose
Anser anser
To 33 in. (83 cm)
Widespread winter visitor.

Taiga Bean Goose
Anser fabalis
To 33 in. (83 cm)

Barnacle Goose
Branta leucopsis
To 28 in. (70 cm)

Canada Goose
Branta canadensis
To 45 in. (1.14 m)

Common Shelduck
Tadorna tadorna
To 26 in. (65 cm)

Great Cormorant
Phalacrocorax carbo
To 38 in. (95 cm)
Note large size and white patch on leg.

Mallard
Anas platyrhynchos To 26 in. (65 cm)

Green-winged Teal
Anas crecca To 15 in. (38 cm)

Common Goldeneye
Bucephala clangula To 18 in. (45 cm)
Male has a white facial spot.

Common Pochard
Aythya ferina To 18 in. (45 cm)

Tufted Duck
Aythya fuligula To 17 in. (43 cm)
Note prominent head crest.

Scaup
Aythya marila To 20 in. (50 cm)
Note rounded head.

Common Eider
Somateria mollissima To 28 in. (70 cm)
Note sloping head profile.

Common Scoter
Melanitta nigra To 19 in. (48 cm)

Eurasian Coot
Fulica atra
To 16 in. (40 cm)

Red-breasted Merganser
Mergus serrator To 27 in. (68 cm)
Note prominent head crest.

Common Merganser
Mergus merganser
To 27 in. (68 cm)
Note thin bill.

Eurasian Wigeon
Mareca penelope To 20 in. (50 cm)

Gray Heron
Ardea cinerea
To 38 in. (95 cm)

Common Murre
Uria aalge
To 18 in. (45 cm)

Common Crane
Grus grus
To 4 ft. (1.2 m)

Pied Avocet
Recurvirostra avosetta
To 18 in. (45 cm)

Eurasian Moorhen
Gallinula chloropus
To 14 in. (35 cm)

Black Guillemot
Cepphus grylle
To 14 in. (35 cm)

Razorbill
Alca torda
To 18 in. (45 cm)

Water Rail
Rallus aquaticus
To 11 in. (28 cm)
Note red bill and barred flanks.

Eurasian Oystercatcher
Haematopus ostralegus
To 18 in. (45 cm)

Eurasian Curlew
Numenius arquata
To 25 in. (63 cm)

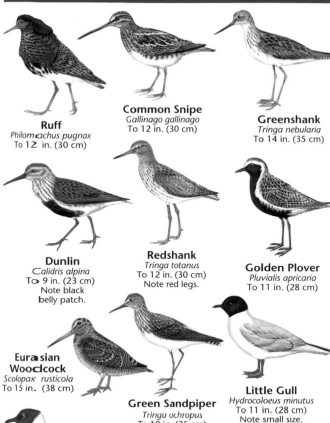

Northern Lapwing
Vanellus vanellus
To 12 in. (30 cm)

Ringed Plover
Charadrius hiaticula
To 8 in. (20 cm)

Little Ringed Plover
Charadrius dubius
To 6 in. (15 cm)

Ruff
Philomachus pugnax
To 12 (30 cm)

Common Snipe
Gallinago gallinago
To 12 in. (30 cm)

Greenshank
Tringa nebularia
To 14 in. (35 cm)

Dunlin
Calidris alpina
To 9 in. (23 cm)
Note black belly patch.

Redshank
Tringa totanus
To 12 in. (30 cm)
Note red legs.

Golden Plover
Pluvialis apricaria
To 11 in. (28 cm)

Eurasian Woodcock
Scolopax rusticola
To 15 in. (38 cm)

Green Sandpiper
Tringa ochropus
To 10 in. (25 cm)

Little Gull
Hydrocoloeus minutus
To 11 in. (28 cm)
Note small size.

Black-headed Gull
Chroicocephalus ridibundus
To 18 in. (45 cm)

Mew Gull
Larus canus
To 18 in. (45 cm)
Note small size.
Legs are yellowish.

Common Tern
Sterna hirundo
To 15 in. (38 cm)
Orange bill is black-tipped.

Great Black-backed Gull
Larus marinus
To 32 in. (80 cm)
Told by large size and dark back.

Herring Gull
Larus argentatus
To 26 in. (65 cm)
Wing tips are black with white spots.
Legs are pinkish.

Sandwich Tern
Thalasseus sandvicensis
To 18 in. (45 cm)
Black bill is yellow-tipped.

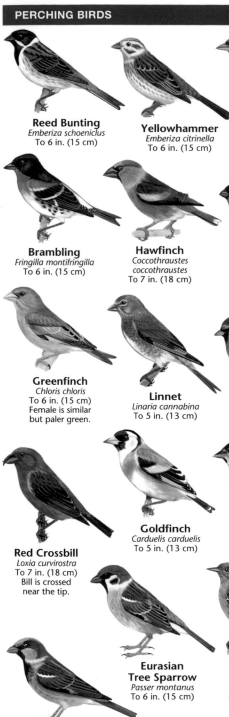

DOVES, WOODPECKERS, ETC.

Rock Pigeon
Columba livia
To 13 in. (33 cm)

Stock Dove
Columba oenas
To 13 in. (33 cm)

Woodpigeon
Columba palumbus
To 17 in. (43 cm)
Note white neck mark.

Eurasian Collared-Dove
Streptopelia decaocto
To 11 in. (28 cm)
Note dark band on nape.

Common Kingfisher
Alcedo atthis
To 7 in. (18 cm)

Common Cuckoo
Cuculus canorus
To 14 in. (35 cm)
Plumage is either gray or red-brown.

Black Woodpecker
Dryocopus martinus
To 18 in. (45 cm)

Green Woodpecker
Picus viridis
To 13 in. (33 cm)

Lesser Spotted Woodpecker
Dryobates minor
To 6 in. (15 cm)

Great Spotted Woodpecker
Dendrocopos major
To 10 in. (25 cm)
Note reddish undertail feathers.

Willow Ptarmigan
Lagopus lagopus
To 15 in. (38 cm)
Plumage is white in winter. Also called willow grouse.

Gray Partridge
Perdix perdix
To 14 in. (35 cm)
Note 'U'-shaped belly patch.

Ring-necked Pheasant
Phasianus colchicus
To 3 ft. (90 cm)

Common Swift
Apus apus
To 7 in. (18 cm)

BIRDS OF PREY

Osprey
Pandion haliaetus
To 2 ft. (60 cm)
Fish-eating raptor.

Golden Eagle
Aquila chrysaetos
To 40 in. (1 m)

Eurasian Marsh Harrier
Circus aeruginosus
To 23 in. (58 cm)

Hen Harrier
Circus cyaneus
To 22 in. (55 cm)

Sparrowhawk
Accipiter nisus
To 16 in. (40 cm)

Northern Goshawk
Accipiter gentilis
To 27 in. (68 cm)

White-tailed Sea Eagle
Haliaeetus albicilla
To 37 in. (93 cm)

Common Kestrel
Falco tinnunculus
To 14 in. (35 cm)

Red Kite
Milvus milvus
To 26 in. (65 cm)
Note deeply-forked reddish tail.

Rough-legged Hawk
Buteo lagopus
To 2 ft. (60 cm)
Note dark 'wrists'.

Black Kite
Milvus migrans
To 22 in. (55 cm)
Note flash of white on underwings.

Common Buzzard
Buteo buteo
To 22 in. (55 cm)

Peregrine Falcon
Falco peregrinus
To 20 in. (50 cm)

Eurasian Pygmy Owl
Glaucidium passerinum
To 8 in. (20 cm)

Tawny Owl
Strix aluco
To 16 in. (40 cm)

PERCHING BIRDS

Great Gray Shrike
Lanius excubitor
To 10 in. (25 cm)

Eurasian Jay
Garrulus glandarius
To 14 in. (35 cm)

Eurasian Magpie
Pica pica
To 18 in. (45 cm)

Jackdaw
Corvus monedula
To 14 in. (35 cm)

Hooded Crow
Corvus corone cornix
To 20 in. (50 cm)

Rook
Corvus frugilegus
To 18 in. (45 cm)
Note gray patch at base of beak.

Common Raven
Corvus corax
To 30 in. (75 cm)
Note large size and heavy bill.

Common Blackbird
Turdus merula
To 10 in. (25 cm)
National bird of Sweden.

European Starling
Sturnus vulgaris
To 8 in. (20 cm)

Barn Swallow
Hirundo rustica
To 8 in. (20 cm)
Note deeply forked tail.

Sand Martin
Riparia riparia
To 6 in. (15 cm)
Note breast band.

Coal Tit
Periparus ater
To 5 in. (13 cm)
Note white nape.

Great Tit
Parus major
To 6 in. (15 cm)
Note black stripe down center of breast.

Willow Tit
Poecile montanus
To 5 in. (13 cm)

Marsh Tit
Poecile palustris
To 5 in. (13 cm)

PERCHING BIRDS

Crested Tit
Lophophanes cristatus
To 5 in. (13 cm)

Nuthatch
Sitta europea
To 6 in. (15 cm)
Often seen crawling along tree trunks in search of insects.

Treecreeper
Certhia familiaris
To 5 in. (13 cm)
Usually seen foraging for insects on tree trunks.

Winter Wren
Troglodytes troglodytes
To 4 in. (10 cm)

Willow Warbler
Phylloscopus trochilus
To 5 in. (13 cm)

Goldcrest
Regulus regulus
To 4 in. (10 cm)
Tiny woodland bird.

Wood Warbler
Phylloscopus sibilatrix
To 5 in. (13 cm)

Blackcap
Sylvia atricapilla
To 6 in. (15 cm)

Chiffchaff
Phylloscopus collybita
To 4 in. (10 cm)

Garden Warbler
Sylvia borin
To 6 in. (15 cm)

Lesser Whitethroat
Sylvia curruca
To 5 in. (13 cm)

Common Whitethroat
Sylvia communis
To 6 in. (15 cm)

Spotted Flycatcher
Muscicapa striata
To 6 in. (15 cm)
Flicks its tail while perching.

Pied Flycatcher
Ficedula hypoleuca
To 5 in. (13 cm)

European Robin
Erithacus rubecula
To 5 in. (13 cm)

PERCHING BIRDS

Redstart
Phoenicurus phoenicurus
To 6 in. (15 cm)

Whinchat
Saxicola rubetra
To 5 in. (13 cm)

Northern Wheatear
Oenanthe oenanthe
To 6 in. (15 cm)

Fieldfare
Turdus pilaris
To 10 in. (25 cm)

Bohemian Waxwing
Bombycilla garrulus
To 8 in. (20 cm)
Red wing marks look like waxy droplets.

Redwing
Turdus iliacus
To 9 in. (23 cm)

Song Thrush
Turdus philomelos
To 9 in. (23 cm)
Calls and songs are highly variable.

Mistle Thrush
Turdus viscivorus
To 11 in. (28 cm)
Back is gray-brown.

Eurasian Skylark
Alauda arvensis
To 7 in. (18 cm)
Known for the long-lasting, melodious song the male gives on the wing.

Yellow Wagtail
Motacilla flava
To 6 in. (15 cm)

White Wagtail
Motacilla alba
To 8 in. (20 cm)
Constantly wags its tail when foraging on the ground.

Meadow Pipit
Anthus pratensis
To 6 in. (15 cm)
Common in open, treeless habitats.

Tree Pipit
Anthus trivialis
To 6 in. (15 cm)

Snow Bunting
Plectrophenax nivalis
To 8 in. (20 cm)

Bearded Reeding
Panurus biarmicus
To 6 in. (15 cm)

PERCHING BIRDS

Reed Bunting
Emberiza schoeniclus
To 6 in. (15 cm)

Yellowhammer
Emberiza citrinella
To 6 in. (15 cm)

Chaffinch
Fringilla coelebs
To 6 in. (15 cm)
Note white shoulders.

Brambling
Fringilla montifringilla
To 6 in. (15 cm)

Hawfinch
Coccothraustes coccothraustes
To 7 in. (18 cm)

Eurasian Bullfinch
Pyrrhula pyrrhula
To 6 in. (15 cm)

Greenfinch
Chloris chloris
To 6 in. (15 cm)
Female is similar but paler green.

Linnet
Linaria cannabina
To 5 in. (13 cm)

Common Redpoll
Acanthis flammea
To 5 in. (13 cm)

Red Crossbill
Loxia curvirostra
To 7 in. (18 cm)
Bill is crossed near the tip.

Goldfinch
Carduelis carduelis
To 5 in. (13 cm)

Siskin
Spinus spinus
To 5 in. (13 cm)

Eurasian Tree Sparrow
Passer montanus
To 6 in. (15 cm)

Dunnock (Hedge Sparrow)
Prunella modularis
To 6 in. (15 cm)
Note gray on head and breast.

House Sparrow
Passer domesticus
To 6 in. (15 cm)